CLEVELAND

A Portrait of the City

PHOTOGRAPHS BY

Jonathan Wayne

GRAY & COMPANY, PUBLISHERS

CLEVELAND

Preface

Cleveland is a challenging subject for a portrait. Size alone makes it impossible to capture in a single image. Unusual diversity adds to its complexity. Greater Cleveland includes over a thousand square miles and combines, for example, the arts of University Circle and the industry of the Flats, downtown's striking commercial architecture and the surrounding Metroparks' natural preserves, old urban neighborhoods and luxurious suburbs, lakefront and lowlands and heights—all of it split nearly down the middle by the Cuyahoga River. And unlike more traditional portrait subjects, there's no way to get a city to stand still. It is constantly moving, it continues to grow, and it changes—throughout the day and throughout the seasons.

My goal was to create a collection of images that would be a composite portrait of the city. More than just a collection, it would be a selection—a sample—gathered in the way an anthropologist might assemble artifacts to portray a larger picture. To be practical and useful as a book, it would need to be an *efficient* sample, too.

If the process was like collecting, it was a little like fishing, as well. It required the right equipment, patience, awareness of surroundings and possibilities, the right weather, and some luck. After making an initial selection of subjects to photograph from the numerous distinct and intriguing elements that make up greater Cleveland, I approached each in the same manner I would any other portrait subject. First, get to know its features. Then, learn about its background. And finally, without imposing upon the subject, decide which attributes to let in through the lens. After the creation of almost three thousand transparencies of several hundred subjects, the selection process began again—and again—until finally the sample was reduced to the one hundred images included here.

This portrait aims to portray Cleveland on many levels. First, there is the recognizable city distilled into a select hundred photographs. In the details, there is much more—new things for viewers to see, and familiar things to be seen in new ways. And the result should exceed the sum of its photographic parts. If it does, perhaps it will reflect, for life-long Clevelanders and newcomers alike, not only this rich and varied city, but also something about their place in it, and its place in them.

[Notes to the photographs begin on page 91.]

North Coast Harbor, site of the Rock and Roll Hall of Fame and Museum
and the Great Lakes Science Center.

A Mckee Sons freighter in the docks
of the AKZO Salt Co. on Whiskey Island.

A historic Public Square street light adorns
the Society National Bank building.

The Free Speech quadrant of Public Square
honors Tom L. Johnson, former mayor of Cleveland.

Fountain of the Waters, at the Cleveland Museum of Art in University Circle.

Night Passing Earth to Day overlooks Wade Lagoon
and the Fine Arts Garden.

Downtown Cleveland's evening skyline, from
Edgewater State Park on the city's west side.

The Art-Deco-style Westlake building towers above the
Cleveland Yacht Club on the Rocky River.

Lemko Hall in the Tremont district, one of Cleveland's oldest neighborhoods.

Free Stamp plays tricks with scale from
        its toppled position in Willard Park.

The Old Stone Church, oldest building on Public Square.

The Epworth Euclid United Church casts an evening shadow over Wade Lagoon
in University Circle.

Lake View Cemetery is the final resting place of many important Clevelanders, including John D. Rockefeller and his family.

Metroparks Rocky River Reservation.

The Terminal Tower, from the northeast quadrant of Public Square.

The Cleveland Orchestra plays to summer crowds at Blossom Music Center.

A floating museum, the Steamer William G. Mather
is docked at the North Coast Inner Harbor.

The evening skyline seen from Erieview Tower.

Sunset over Lake Erie, from Lakewood Park.

Architectural details from around the city.

The Armor Court, housed in the oldest building of the Cleveland Museum of Art.

Details of the old Art Deco main post office
are preserved in the lobby of the M K-Ferguson Plaza.

The City of Culture Fountain is the centerpiece
of the Stouffer Tower City Plaza Hotel lobby.

U.S.S. COD, sole remaining authentic WWII American sub,
is permanently moored on Cleveland's lakefront.

The multifaceted Rock and Roll Hall of Fame and
Museum building juts out into North Coast Harbor.

The city's eastern lakefront and skyline, from Society Tower.

Lakeside Yacht Club, looking west toward downtown.

St. Christopher's-by-the-River in Gates Mills.

Chagrin Falls Village, centered on the
Chagrin River 18 miles east of Cleveland.

One of the many distinguished homes along
Fairmount Boulevard in Cleveland Heights.

The Metroparks toboggan run at Mill Stream Run Reservation in Strongsville.

A European-style market hall, the West Side Market
caters to a variety of ethnic traditions.

Many West Side Market vendors have operated
the same stands for generations.

The Arcade, a century-old thoroughfare
under a hundred-foot high atrium of steel and glass.

The Avenue at Tower City fills with color during the holidays.

A Great Lakes freighter unloading gravel in the Flats.

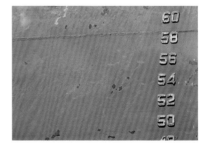

The crooked Cuyahoga near its mouth
on Lake Erie, from the Society Tower.

The four-story Skylight Concourse covers The Avenue
at Tower City between Huron and Prospect Avenues.

Public sculpture enlivens the urban campus of Cleveland State University.

The 52-story Terminal Tower, from the Society Tower.

Triple L Eccentric Gyratory III swings
    in the breeze at East 9th Street and Euclid Avenue.

Two eras of Cleveland skyscrapers and the Old Stone
Church anchor the north side of Public Square.

The skyline, looking toward Collision Bend on the Cuyahoga River.

Winter steam rises in front of the
    Old Federal Building at East 3rd and Superior.

Winter fog settles over Edgewater State Park.

One of four sculptures representing the seasons
on the lawn of the Rockefeller Park Greenhouse.

The Cleveland Ballet performing at the State Theatre in Playhouse Square.

Pleasure boaters arrive for an evening's entertainment
on the banks of the Cuyahoga River in the Flats.

The Beaux-Arts Cuyahoga County Courthouse
viewed through Isamu Noguchi's modernist *Portal*.

Sculptural architectural details from around the city.

Sunset on Lake Erie silhouettes the historic
Hulett ore unloaders on Whiskey Island.

The Holden Arboretum shows off its Autumn colors.

The skyline seen from the Cuyahoga River, heading upstream.

Crewing on the Cuyahoga.

City founder Moses Cleaveland, in bronze, stands with
his surveyor's equipment overlooking Public Square.

Snowstorm in Wade Park Lagoon.

Spring brings color to Willard Park despite a lakefront fog.

The lily pond at The Garden Center of Greater Cleveland.

Skyline and a light breeze off the lake, from Edgewater State Park.

Georgian and Tudor Revival styles are common
along tree-lined Clifton Boulevard in Lakewood.

Victorian houses abound in the Ohio City
neighborhood of Cleveland's near west side.

The courtyard of the Hanna Mansion, part of
the Western Reserve Historical Society in University Circle.

The Cleveland Museum of Art,
from the Fine Arts Gardens in Wade Park.

Glidden House, a historic mansion turned elegant
University Circle bed-and-breakfast.

The Shaker Lakes Regional Nature Center protects
and displays a fertile marshland in close proximity to the city.

The exhibits of the Metroparks Zoo feature world-wide wildlife only five miles from downtown.

One of a range of horticultural displays
under glass in the city's Rockefeller Park Greenhouse.

The courtyard of the Galleria at Erieview, off East 9th Street

The 888-foot Society Tower rises above Public Square
and the silhouette of the Soldiers and Sailors Monument.

One of four massive pylons—the Guardians of Traffic—marking the corners of the Hope Memorial Bridge.

St. Patrick Roman Catholic Church,
a distinctive Ohio City Victorian.

The Chagrin River flows peacefully near
the town of Gates Mills, east of Cleveland.

Downtown Cleveland alive with lights, from the Erieview Tower.

NOTES

Text by Christopher Johnston

North Coast Harbor at Sunset
East 9th and Erieside Avenue
Comprising 176 acres of lakefront property, North Coast Harbor serves as home to the Rock and Roll Hall of Fame and Museum, the Great Lakes Science Center, Voinovich Park, and the Steamship *William G. Mather* Museum. Known as the Inner Harbor until 1987, North Coast Harbor's development was a vital component of Cleveland's downtown and lakefront revitalization.

Freighter Docked at Whiskey Island
Shown in the docks of the AKZO Salt Co. on Whiskey Island, this McKee Sons freighter is typical of the Great Lakes ships that frequent Cleveland's ports. Owned by the Upper Lakes Barge Co., this particular craft measures 655 feet in length and 71 feet in width, with a draft of 25 feet, 7 inches and a capacity of 21,000 tons.

**Society National Bank,
BP America Building**
Public Square
Known as the Society for Savings Building until 1970, the former headquarters of Society National Bank displays one of Public Square's historic street lights. The corner bracket fixture, believed to have been designed by inventor Charles F. Brush, contained the first incandescent light on the Square. In the background is a more recent addition to the skyline, the broad-shouldered BP America Building (1985). Enclosing 1.2 million square feet of office space, the 45-story, 650-foot-tall BP Building is clad with glazed red granite.

Statue of Tom L. Johnson
Public Square, northwest quadrant
Tom L. Johnson, populist mayor (1901-1909) and civic reformer, was commemorated with this statue in 1915. Sculpted by Herman N. Matzer, it reposes in the middle of what is popularly referred to as the Free Speech quadrant of Public Square, in honor of Johnson's frequent use of public meetings. Here, the statue is framed by the Old Stone Church and 75 Public Square (1915), an angular 15-story building that was the first headquarters of the Cleveland Electric Illuminating Co.

***Fountain of the Waters*, Fine Arts Garden**
Wade Oval, University Circle
Located in the Court of Nature section of the Fine Arts Garden, the *Fountain of the Waters* by Chester Beach is a refreshing sight on a hot summer evening in University Circle. The fountain's two main figure groups represent the flowing waters of rivers into lakes, while the figures of children on the sides symbolize the flowers by the banks of the rivers.

Wade Park Lagoon, Fine Arts Garden
University Circle
The statue of *Night Passing Earth To Day* by Cleveland sculptor Frank L. Jirouch greets pedestrians who enter the Fine Arts Garden from Euclid Avenue. The central Lagoon is surrounded by several garden areas, including a stand of unusual European-style flat-topped sycamores that remain from the original landscape design of 1916.

Skyline from Edgewater State Park

The Westlake
19000 Lake Road, Rocky River
Rocky River's most eye-catching landmark was built in 1925 as The Westlake Hotel. An example of early Art Deco design, the Westlake was considered a luxury residential hotel. In 1983, a complete renovation turned the historic hotel into a condominium complex. This view from the Norfolk & Southern Bridge overlooks the Cleveland Yacht Club, founded in 1878.

Lemko Hall
West 11th Street and Literary Avenue
Situated in the Tremont District of Cleveland, Lemko Hall (1911) was once the home of the Cleveland Branch of the Lemko Association, a social club established in 1929 to serve immigrants from the Slavic country of Lemkovina. The hall made a guest appearance in the 1977 film *The Deer Hunter* as the locale for the wedding feast scenes. It has been restored and converted to retail space and loft apartments.

***Free Stamp*, North Point Tower**
St. Clair Avenue and East 9th Street
This sculpture by Claes Oldenburg and his wife, Coosje van Bruggen, has provoked curiosity, controversy, and discussion since it was commissioned in 1985. Originally intended for a spot on Public Square, the statue languished in storage for six years after BP America, Inc. rejected it, then donated it to the city. In November of 1991, *Free Stamp* finally came to rest in a toppled position in Willard Park outside of Cleveland City Hall. Immediately behind the statue is North Point Tower, built on the foundations of the Cleveland Press building and completed in 1990.

Old Stone Church
Ontario Street and Public Square
The First Presbyterian Church is one of the oldest buildings downtown. The original house of worship, completed in 1833, became known as the Old Stone Church because it was constructed of Berea sandstone. The present exterior remains from a later building,

completed in 1857. Many notable Clevelanders have attended services at the church, and today it still serves a sizable and active congregation.

Wade Park Lagoon
University Circle
At the heart of University Circle, Wade Park Lagoon reflects the gracious landscaping of the Art Museum's Fine Arts Garden. In the foreground is the Epworth Euclid United Methodist Church. The distinctive dome and spire of this familiar landmark lead to its popular nickname, the Oil Can Church.

**Rockefeller Monument,
Lake View Cemetery**
12316 Euclid Avenue, East Cleveland
At the base of this obelisk lie the remains of oil magnate John D. Rockefeller and his family. Known for its rolling, landscaped lawns and gardens and its magnificent memorial architecture, Lake View Cemetery is also the final resting place of many of the city's most famous residents, including the Van Sweringens, Marcus Hanna, Charles Brush, Alexander Winton, and Jeptha Wade, who helped found the cemetery in 1869. Situated atop a forested bluff east of Cleveland, the park-like cemetery acquired its name because of the expansive vistas.

Rocky River Reservation
The Rocky River Reservation is the largest 'gem' in the Cleveland Metroparks' Emerald Necklace (so named because the string of parks nearly encircles the city). From Lakewood southeast to Strongsville, this reservation runs the length of the Rocky River Valley, offering a natural setting for a wide range of recreation and providing numerous scenic overlooks.

Public Square, northeast quadrant
The four quadrants of Public Square, each approximately one acre in size, possess distinctive characters. The northeast quadrant shown here is extensively landscaped with trees and shrubs and is bisected by two footpaths, one of which is on an axis with the Terminal Tower.

Cleveland Orchestra in Summer
Blossom Music Center, Cuyahoga Falls
One of the world's finest orchestras has been performing in Cleveland since 1918. Early Orchestra performances were held at Masonic Auditorium and Music Hall. In 1931, the Orchestra moved to its permanent home, Severance Hall, which was built with funds provided by philanthropist John L. Severence. Since 1968, an annual summer series of concerts has been held at Blossom Music

Center, tucked in the wooded hills of the Cuyahoga Valley National Recreation Area between Cleveland and Akron. The Orchestra's reputation has grown as a result of several foreign tours and many outstanding commercial recordings.

PAGE 25
Steamship *William G. Mather* Museum
East 9th Street Pier
This restored Great Lakes ore carrier, which retired from service in 1980, is now a maritime museum docked at North Coast Harbor. The 618-foot-long, 8,662-ton vessel, named for community and industrial leader William Gwinn Mather, was built in 1925 as the flagship of the Cleveland-Cliffs Iron Company. The freighter averaged 30 trips per season, hauling iron ore to the industrial centers of the Great Lakes. Four cargo holds could carry up to 13,300 tons. In 1995, the Harbor Heritage Soc. was created to oversee the operation and restoration of the *Mather*.

PAGE 26
Skyline from Erieview Tower
This view from Erieview Tower frames the three key buildings that mark the corners of Public Square. The lower center of the photo also displays the south end of Mall A, a part of the city's historic Group Plan initiated in 1903 and developed over the next 30 years. One Cleveland Center—"the silver chisel building"—(lower left) was erected on East 9th Street in 1983.

PAGE 27
Lakewood Park
Lake Avenue at Belle Avenue, Lakewood
Residents of this suburb immediately west of Cleveland regularly enjoy panoramic vistas of Lake Erie from Lakewood Park.

PAGE 28
Detail, War Memorial Fountain
Mall A, between St. Clair Avenue and Rockwell Avenue
At the center of the War Memorial Fountain stands a bronze sphere, 10-1/2 feet in diameter, meant to symbolize the superstitions and legends of man.

Detail, James A. Garfield Monument
Lake View Cemetery, 12316 Euclid Avenue, East Cleveland
James A. Garfield's Tomb was built in 1890 as a monument to the slain President. Garfield (1831-1881), who was born in Orange Township and resided in Mentor, lies at rest inside the elaborately decorated memorial. The monument, 180 feet in height and 50 feet in diameter, offers a sweeping view of Lake Erie and Cleveland's East Side.

Detail of ceiling, Federal Reserve Bank of Cleveland
East 6th Street and Superior Avenue
One of 12 banks in the U.S. Federal Reserve System, the Cleveland Fed is housed in a building designed by the prestigious architectural firm of Walker & Weeks. Modeled after the Medici palace in Florence, the building's magnificent interior features a vaulted ceiling with gilt ornamentation.

Detail, The Cleveland Clinic Building
East 100th Street and Euclid Avenue
This striking, award-winning structure—14 stories of granite and glass commonly referred to as "the ziggurat building"—was designed by Cesar Pelli, the architect responsible for Society Tower. Erected in 1985, it serves as the main building for the internationally-acclaimed Cleveland Clinic.

PAGE 29
Armor Court, Cleveland Museum of Art
Wade Oval, University Circle
Located in the original museum building (1916), the Armor Court exhibits a collection of armor donated by philanthropist John L. Severance. At the time, an exhibit of armor was unusual in an American museum, but it was considered appropriate for "industrial Cleveland" and expected to be "of interest to metal workers of every degree." The 34-foot-high gallery is lined with 17th century tapestries from the Barbarini Palace. The piece in the foreground is *Cornwall Circle*, by Richard Long.

PAGE 30
Interior of M K-Ferguson Plaza
Prospect Avenue NW and West 6th Street
Erected in 1934 as the last building in the historic Terminal Tower Group, this building served as Cleveland's Main Post Office until 1983. During development of Tower City Center, it was restored as a corporate office building. The imposing 228-foot-long lobby—now the only public space in the half-million-square-foot building—still features the classic Art Deco postal windows and customer counters.

Detail, M K-Ferguson Plaza
This detail in the wall of the old post office lobby depicts a forerunner of the U.S. mail system: the stagecoach driver, who was responsible for carrying packages and letters along his route.

PAGE 31
Stouffer Tower City Plaza Hotel
Public Square
The first hotel on this site was an inn built in 1812. The present 12-story, 500-room hotel was completed in 1929 as part of the Van Sweringens' Terminal Tower project; it is a charter member of the Historic Hotels of America. The final phase of a comprehensive refurbishment program completed in 1991 was Stouffer's regal lobby with its vaulted ceilings and white marble centerpiece, rededicated as the City of Culture Fountain.

PAGE 32
Cleveland National Air Show
Burke Lakefront Airport
A long-standing tradition for Labor Day Weekend, the air show lets people get close to amazing civilian and military aircraft. This festival of flight is one of the largest in the country, and it features spectacular demonstrations by daring stunt pilots. The current show was first held in 1964. It is a descendant of the National Air Races, held here from 1929-1949, which drew many of the greatest aviators of all time.

U.S.S. *Cod*
1089 East 9th Street
Permanently moored on Cleveland's lakefront, the *Cod* allows visitors to experience cramped quarters that were home to 155 officers and crew during World War II. The U.S. Navy submersible (unlike a true submarine, it can only dive under water for short periods of time) operated in the South Pacific, where it sank 10 Japanese warships and 30 merchant ships. The sub was moved here in 1959 to serve as a training ship and, in 1976, the *Cod* was donated to the city of Cleveland. The last remaining authentic WWII American sub, it is now listed in the National Register of Historic Ships.

PAGE 33
Rock and Roll Hall of Fame and Museum
1 Key Plaza, Erieside Avenue
Designed by renowned architect I.M. Pei and opened in 1995, the Rock and Roll Hall of Fame and Museum is the centerpiece of North Coast Harbor. The building houses the Hall of Inductees and four floors of display collections, short films, and interactive listening stands that trace the heritage of rock music and its impact on American and global culture.

PAGE 34
Freighter unloading in The Flats
Equipped with its own unloading machinery, this boat filled with taconite is docked near the famous Hulett unloaders. Invented by Clevelander George H. Hulett in the early part of the century, these innovative devices that significantly impacted the ore shipping industry have given way to more modern technology.

PAGE 35
Parade of Lights
Cuyahoga River, The Flats
In July, a brilliant Parade of Lights opens the annual Flats festival. Dozens of boaters compete for prizes in a winding procession from the mouth of the Cuyahoga River to Collision Bend. Here, the Powerhouse provides a massive backdrop with its immense arches and 240-foot-high chimneys. Built in 1892 by industrialist and philanthropist Marcus A. Hanna to supply electricity for streetcars, the Powerhouse was restored and converted into an entertainment and retail facility in 1989.

PAGE 36
Cleveland skyline and lakefront
Skyline and city stretch east along the lakefront, viewed here from the Society Tower. Prominent buildings include, from left to right, the Federal Building, Ohio Bell Building, Erieview Tower and the Galleria, and One Cleveland Center.

PAGE 37
Lakeside Yacht Club
4851 North Marginal Road
Founded in 1930 at the East 9th Street Pier, Lakeside Yacht Club moved to its present location in 1932. The facility includes a clubhouse and 260 boat slips. Each year, the club sponsors the LYC Regatta, Firecracker Race, and Governor's Cup and Mayor's Races.

Triple L Eccentric Gyratory III
East 9th Street and Euclid Avenue
This kinetic sculpture, created by George Rickey, slowly swings in the heart of Cleveland's financial district.

Society Tower, Society National Bank, Old Stone Church
Public Square
Two eras of Cleveland skyscrapers are represented side by side: the Society Tower (1991) rises high above the Society National Bank building (1890). Landmark edifice and sleek modern tower are linked at ground level in the Society Center development. Nearby stands the Old Stone Church (1857), the oldest building on Public Square.

Detail, Society National Bank
Dramatic red sandstone walls, five feet thick at the corners, reinforce the solidity and stability of the 10-story building. Architect John Wellborn Root designed the massive exterior to resemble an indestructible medieval fortress in which a working man's money would be safe.

Skyline from Collision Bend
Collision Bend was the most hazardous part of the Cuyahoga River before it was widened in the late 1930s. The name is derived from the many boat collisions that occurred in its sharp and narrow turn. Despite the opening of a more direct channel to Lake Erie in 1827 (which created Whiskey Island), river traffic jammed the Cuyahoga during the city's 19th-century emergence as a commercial center. By 1881, industry occupied nearly all riverfront property along the Cuyahoga's twisting journey through the Flats to the lakefront.

Old Federal Building
Superior Avenue and East 3rd Street
Icy winds whipping off Lake Erie call for a brisk pace downtown in winter. Behind the steam on this corner stands the Old Federal Building. Used today primarily as a federal court house, this building contained the U.S. Post Office, Custom House, and Court House when it opened in 1910.

Edgewater State Park
On the lakefront, between West 58th Street and West 103rd Street
Here, a winter fog settles over Edgewater State Park. The property was purchased by the city in 1894 from Cleveland industrialist Jacob B. Perkins. By 1978, Edgewater became one of three components of the Cleveland Lakefront State Park. Edgewater has served as the site of the city's annual 4th of July Festival of Freedom since 1954.

Sculpture, Rockefeller Park Greenhouse
780 East 88th Street
One of a set of sculptures representing the four seasons, the beauty of this statues is enhanced by the seasonal splendor surrounding them on the landscaped lawn area in front of the greenhouse. The sculptures were donated by a private estate in the early 1960s.

Cleveland Ballet
State Theatre, 1501 Euclid Avenue, Playhouse Square
Since its first public appearance at the Hanna Theatre in November of 1976, the Cleveland Ballet has established a national reputation for superior performances. The company's lavish production of the classic ballet *Swan Lake*, pictured here, sparkles with 135 gracious costumes and equally splendid sets. In 1984, the Cleveland Ballet moved to its present home in the newly restored State Theatre in Playhouse Square.

The Flats, Cuyahoga River
At the mouth of the Cuyahoga River lies the Flats District, 620 acres of prime riverfront flatland that is the shipping and manufacturing center of the city's steel, iron, lumber, chemical, oil, flour, and salt industries. In the 1980s, a large area of the Flats was revived as one of Cleveland's major entertainment centers. Pleasure boaters often dock at the bars and restaurants that flank the river. The Main Avenue high-level bridge, which towers above, was built in 1939.

Portal and Cuyahoga County Courthouse
Cuyahoga County Justice Center
Funded by the George Gund Foundation and installed in 1976, this 15-ton, 36-foot-high carbon-steel pipe sculpture by Isamu Noguchi sits at the Ontario Street entrance to the Cuyahoga County Justice Center (completed in 1977). Although controversial because of its conceptual, non-representational style, *Portal* was the first modernist sculptural work to reside among downtown's more classical Beaux-Arts public buildings. Among those is the neighboring Cuyahoga County Courthouse on Lakeside Avenue. Opened in 1912 after seven years of construction, the courthouse was the first building designed as a part of Daniel Burnham's historic Group Plan for the city.

Detail, Cleveland Public Library
325 Superior Avenue
This figure on the front wall of the library was fashioned by the Fischer & Jirouch Company of Cleveland. Since February 17, 1869, the library has provided free access to books and information, evolving into one of the nation's major urban library systems, with nearly 50 miles of shelving.

Detail, Society National Bank Building
Whimsical exterior carvings add a lighter touch to this otherwise intimidating steel-and-masonry building.

Detail, Cuyahoga County Court House
Out of respect for the many tribes who called the shores of Lake Erie home before the arrival of Moses Cleaveland, the bronze doors of the courthouse feature an exquisitely molded Indian Chief's head with feathered headdress. The doors open to an equally ornate interior.

Detail, Rockefeller Park Greenhouse
This striking lineup of gargoyles adorns a wall outside of the greenhouse entrance. The wall was donated to the facility when the Pennsylvania Railroad Station at 55th Street and Euclid Avenue was demolished.

Hulett Unloaders on Whiskey Island
The gigantic cantilevered arms of George H. Hulett's ore-unloaders, built in 1903, symbolize Cleveland's industrial might at the turn of the century. Hulett's ingenious device revolutionized ore shipping on the Great Lakes. The imposing monsters reduced a task—unloading 10,000 tons of ore—that once took 100 men 24 hours to perform to five hours with 25 men. Whiskey Island acquired its moniker in the 1830s after a distillery was erected on the island.

The Holden Arboretum
9500 Sperry Road, Mentor
Holden, at 3,100 acres, is the largest arboretum in the U.S. Its facilities combine scientific research (more than 4,800 different plant species have been identified here) with a natural setting popular for hiking and bird-watching. Horticultural collections include wildflowers, prairie plants, and bogs.

Skyline from the Cuyahoga
Prominent in this view, and just south of Public Square, stands the Landmark Office Towers, comprised of three adjacent buildings: The Midland Building, the Medical Arts (LTV Steel) Building, and the Builders Exchange (Guildhall). The structure was part of the original Van Sweringen Brothers project that developed 17 acres of buildings on 35 acres of land. To the left is the old main post office building, now the M-K Furguson Plaza. In the foreground is the Sherwin Williams Co. research facility.

Crewing on the Cuyahoga River
Vying for space on the river with freighters, tugboats, and pleasure craft, intrepid crewing teams will occasionally be seen gliding along the Cuyahoga. This particular crew is from the Flats Racing Team of the Cleveland Rowing Federation.

Gund Arena and Cleveland Cavaliers
Huron Road and Ontario Street
Cavaliers basketball and Lumberjacks hockey are the two biggest draws at Gund Arena, completed in 1994 as a part of the Gateway Economic Development project. The structure's unusual facade is an intriguing combination of stone, glass, and steel. Named for Cavaliers owners George and Gordon Gund, the state-of-the-art facility hosts a variety of live sports and entertainment events, with a seating capacity of 20,500 spectators.

Jacobs Field and Cleveland Indians
E. 9th Street and Bolivar
Founded in 1901, the Indians were a charter member of the American League, and are one of only four AL teams to have remained in the same city since then. Early on, the Cleveland team had many names, including the Blues, the Broncos, and the Naps (after popular player/ manager Napoleon Lajoie). But in 1915 the name became the Indians, in honor of the American Indian Louis "Chief" Sockalexis, who played for the Cleveland Spiders of the National League in the 1890s. The Tribe plays at home in elegant Jacobs Field, completed for the 1994 season and named for team owner Richard E. Jacobs.

Statue of Bob Feller
Gate C, Jacobs Field
"Rapid Robert" Feller, ace of the Cleveland Indians' pitching staff from 1936–1956, is honored in this Gary Ross sculpture—a popular landmark for fans meeting friends on game day. Feller pitched 3 no-hitters, 12 one-hitters, and struck out 2,581 batters.

Moses Cleaveland Statue
Public Square
This bronze monument to the city's founder was sculpted by James G. C. Hamilton and unveiled in 1888. Cleaveland headed the party of Western Reserve surveyors from the Connecticut Land Co. who landed near the mouth of the Cuyahoga River on July 22, 1796. The Connecticut native laid out the 10-acre Public Square that reflects a traditional New England town plan, while his surveyors planned the city around it and named it for their leader. Cleaveland then returned to his home state in October of 1796 to continue his law practice.

Wade Park Lagoon in Winter
University Circle
Originally part of the 63 acres donated to Cleveland by financier Jeptha Wade in 1882, Wade Park Lagoon presents a beautiful scene year-round. Even a snowstorm cannot obscure the imposing contours of the Epworth Euclid United Methodist Church, completed in 1928. The church's Gothic design is thought to echo Mont St. Michel in France.

Free Stamp
St. Clair Avenue and East 9th Street
A vibrant bed of tulips complements the colorful and controversial statue lying nearby. A 48-foot-long maroon office rubber stamp with bright pink, 18-foot-high letters on its base, *Free Stamp* clearly exemplifies sculptor Claes Oldenburg's trademark creation of monumental replicas of commonplace objects. Behind, from left to right, are the Federal Building, the Cleveland Convention Center, and Cleveland City Hall.

The Garden Center of Greater Cleveland
1130 East Boulevard, University Circle
Established in 1930 and originally located in a boathouse on the Wade Park Lagoon, America's first civic garden center moved to its present facility in 1965. The rustic stone structure houses one of the most extensive public horticulture libraries in the U.S. The grounds of the 6.75-acre property exhibit exceptional herb, rose, wildflower, perennial, and Japanese gardens, as well as the tranquil lily pond.

View from Edgewater State Park
Looking east across Edgewater's grassy meadows and swimming beach offers a great view of downtown. One of the more popular public recreational areas along Cleveland's 12-mile lakefront, Edgewater State Park is used for everything from fishing, swimming, picnicking, and wind surfing in summer to snowball fights and sledding in the winter.

Clifton Boulevard, Lakewood
This sprawling, tree-lined avenue shows off many of Lakewood's stately residences—particularly in autumn. Noted for its friendly, family neighborhoods and strong sense of community, this suburb also prides itself on being a "city of homes." Formally named for its natural setting on Lake Erie in 1889, Lakewood was founded as a village in 1903 and incorporated as a city in 1911. A significant growth spurt in 1917 followed the opening of the Detroit-Superior Bridge.

Jay Street and West 29th Street, Ohio City
Incorporated in 1836 just two days before the City of Cleveland, Ohio City, founded in 1818, carried on a heated rivalry with its neighbor on the east bank of the Cuyahoga River until it was annexed to Cleveland in 1854. The rivalry even erupted into the "Bridge War" of 1836 when, to the dismay of Ohio City, construction of the first permanent bridge over the river stimulated Cleveland's growth. Today, contemporary pioneers are restoring the grand Victorian homes and reviving this historic urban area.

War Memorial Fountain
Mall A, between St. Clair & Rockwell Avenues
Sculpted by Marshall Fredericks, this soaring 35-foot bronze figure represents man escaping the flames of war and reaching for eternal peace. On the surface of the polished granite rim around the *Fountain of Eternal Life*, bronze plates display the names of 4,000 greater Clevelanders who died in World War II and the Korean War.

Holiday Lighting of Public Square
Spectators watch the holiday lighting of Public Square from Cleveland's major Civil War memorial, the Soldiers and Sailors Monument. Designed by Cleveland architect Levi T. Scofield and dedicated on July 4th, 1894, the monument features bronze sculptures on each of its four sides representing the Infantry, Artillery, Cavalry, and Navy. The Society Tower stands in the background.

Detail of Soldiers & Sailors Monument
Inside the monument's Tablet Room, ornately carved stones list the 6,000 Cuyahoga residents who served in the Civil War.

Western Reserve Historical Society
10825 East Boulevard, University Circle
Pictured here is the courtyard of the Hay Mansion, which, along with the Hanna Mansion, comprise the two main buildings of the the Western Reserve Historical Society's museum. Founded in 1867, the society is Cleveland's oldest cultural institution and one of the largest privately-supported historical societies in the country. The facility exhibits a marvelous collection of American furniture, decorative arts, and fashions. It also houses the Frederick C. Crawford Auto-Aviation Museum.

Cleveland Museum of Art
11150 East Boulevard, University Circle
The lushly landscaped Fine Arts Garden (1928) was designed to replace a neglected five-acre parcel south of the Cleveland Museum of Art. Opened to the public on June 6, 1916, the museum has attained a worldwide reputation for excellence. Many of the city's famous benefactors made this cultural jewel a reality, including Jeptha H. Wade I, who donated his Wade Park property for the site of the museum. The Cleveland firm of Hubbell & Benes designed the original neoclassical museum building of white Georgian marble.

Glidden House
1901 Ford Drive, University Circle
Glidden House, now an elegant bed and breakfast, was built in 1910 as the home of Frances Kavanaugh Glidden, son of Frances Harrington Glidden, founder of the Glidden Paint Co. In 1988, a 52-room wing was added to complement the eight luxurious suites in the original mansion.

Shaker Lakes Regional Nature Center
2600 South Park Blvd., Shaker Heights
Open year-round, the nature center is part of the parklands that surround Horseshoe Lake and Lower Lake. These two lakes were formed in the mid-19th century when the Shaker North Union Settlement, a religious community that settled in the area, dammed Doan Brook to power its mills. Since 1983, one of the nature center's most popular attractions has been the All Peoples Trail, an elevated boardwalk that allows visitors to get a bird's-eye view of a fertile marshland ecosystem. The lakes and nature center are a designated National Environmental Educational Landmark.

Cleveland Metroparks Zoo
3900 Brookside Park Drive
Only five miles from downtown, the Zoo offers trips into the wilds of the world: Brazilian spider monkeys, Chilean flamingos, African giraffes, Australian kangaroos, and thousands of other animals inhabit the